# The GOSPEL of JOHN

## Leader Guide

# The Gospel of John
## A Beginner's Guide to the Way, the Truth, and the Life

The Gospel of John
978-1-7910-2792-6
978-1-7910-2795-7 *eBook*

The Gospel of John: DVD
978-1-7910-2794-0

The Gospel of John: Leader Guide
978-1-7910-2793-3
978-1-7910-2796-4 *eBook*

---

## Also by Amy-Jill Levine

*Entering the Passion of Jesus:*
*A Beginner's Guide to Holy Week*

*Light of the World:*
*A Beginner's Guide to Advent*

*Sermon on the Mount:*
*A Beginner's Guide to the Kingdom of Heaven*

*The Difficult Words of Jesus:*
*A Beginner's Guide to His Most Perplexing Teachings*

*The Gospel of Mark:*
*A Beginner's Guide to the Good News*

*Witness at the Cross:*
*A Beginner's Guide to Holy Friday*

*Signs and Wonders:*
*A Beginner's Guide to the Miracles of Jesus*

AMY-JILL LEVINE

A BEGINNER'S GUIDE TO THE WAY, THE TRUTH, AND THE LIFE

# The GOSPEL of JOHN

## LEADER GUIDE

Abingdon Press | Nashville

The Gospel of John:
A Beginner's Guide to the Way, the Truth, and the Life
Leader Guide

978-1-7910-2793-3

MANUFACTURED IN THE UNITED STATES OF AMERICA

# CONTENTS

# CONTENTS

# INTRODUCTION

In *The Gospel of John*, Dr. Amy-Jill Levine (who prefers to go by "AJ") asks probing questions of several stories from the Gospel of John—and of her readers. AJ engages stories of Jesus's encounters with various people, from his mother at a wedding in Cana to Mary Magdalene and Thomas after his resurrection, asking these texts, and those reading them with her, how these stories offer new insights into who Jesus was and is, and what following him today looks like (or ought to look like).

This Leader's Guide is designed to equip volunteers in a congregational setting to lead adult leaders in a six-session study of the texts AJ explores in her book.

Session 1: The Wedding at Cana (John 2)
Session 2: Nicodemus and the Samaritan Woman
at the Well (John 3 & 4)
Session 3: The Healing of the Man at the Pool (John 5)
Session 4: The Man Born Blind (John 9)
Session 5: Foot Washing (John 12 & 13)
Session 6: Mary Magdalene and Doubting Thomas (John 20)

Although this guide contains quotations from AJ's book so that it can be used on its own, leaders and participants will benefit most if they use it with AJ's book.

Each session contains the following elements to draw from as you plan six in-person, virtual, or hybrid sessions:

- Session Goals
- Biblical Foundations—Scripture texts for the session, in the New Revised Standard Version Updated Edition

- Before Your Session—Tips to help you prepare a productive session
- Starting Your Session—Discussion questions intended to "warm up" your group for fruitful discussion
- Opening Prayer
- Book Discussion Questions—You likely will not be able or want to use all the questions in every session, so feel free to pick and choose based on your group's interests and the Spirit's leading.
- Closing Your Session—A focused discussion or reflection, often suggesting action to take beyond the session.
- Closing Prayer
- Optional Extensions (as time and interest allow)

Thank you for your willingness to lead! May you and your group experience a meaningful, challenging, and joyful study of John's Gospel.

# SESSION 1

## The Wedding at Cana

### (John 2)

#### Session Goals

This session includes the introduction's consideration of the Prologue to the Gospel of John. The reading, reflection, discussion, and prayer will help participants:

- understand and articulate ways in which the Prologue to John's Gospel (1:1-18) expresses Jesus's significance through older, scriptural images of creation and light,
- closely read and reflect on the story of Jesus's first sign, turning water into wine at the wedding in Cana (2:1-11), and
- consider and commit to specific ways in which they can together shine as light by "changing what is to something that is better."

#### Biblical Foundations

*In the beginning was the Word, and the Word was with God, and the Word was God. He was in the beginning with God. All things came into being through him, and without him not one thing came into being. What has come into being in him was life, and the life was the light of all people. The light shines in the darkness, and the darkness did not overtake it. . . .*

9

*And the Word became flesh and lived among us, and we have seen his glory, the glory as of a father's only son, full of grace and truth.*

*John 1:1-5, 14*

*On the third day there was a wedding in Cana of Galilee, and the mother of Jesus was there. Jesus and his disciples had also been invited to the wedding. When the wine gave out, the mother of Jesus said to him, "They have no wine." And Jesus said to her, "Woman, what concern is that to me and to you? My hour has not yet come." His mother said to the servants, "Do whatever he tells you." Now standing there were six stone water jars for the Jewish rites of purification, each holding twenty or thirty gallons. Jesus said to them, "Fill the jars with water." And they filled them up to the brim. He said to them, "Now draw some out, and take it to the person in charge of the banquet." So they took it. When the person in charge tasted the water that had become wine and did not know where it came from (though the servants who had drawn the water knew), that person called the bridegroom and said to him, "Everyone serves the good wine first and then the inferior wine after the guests have become drunk. But you have kept the good wine until now." Jesus did this, the first of his signs, in Cana of Galilee and revealed his glory, and his disciples believed in him.*

*John 2:1-11*

## Before Your Session

- Carefully and prayerfully read this session's Biblical Foundations more than once. Note words and phrases that attract your attention and meditate on them. Write down questions you have, and try to answer them, consulting trusted Bible commentaries. Become as familiar with these Scriptures as possible.
- Carefully read the introduction and chapter 1 of AJ's book more than once.
- You will need: either Bibles for in-person participants or screen slides prepared with Scripture texts for sharing (identify the translation used), or both; newsprint or a markerboard and markers (for in-person sessions).

- If using the DVD or streaming video, preview the session 1 video segment. Choose the best time in your session plan for viewing it.

## Starting Your Session

Welcome participants. Tell them why you are excited to study AJ's book with them. Invite them to speak briefly about why they are interested in this study and what they hope to gain from it.

Invite volunteers to share anything they know about the Gospel of John. Write their responses on the newsprint or markerboard. Alternatively, invite participants to spend five minutes skimming the Gospel, then ask them to share brief impressions and reactions.

Tell participants AJ suggests John supplements and "provides his own take" on the Synoptic tradition. John's Gospel is rich in content, and your group will not have time to read and study it all. AJ's book, and your group's study, focus on stories unique to John that can help us appreciate in new ways John's conviction that Jesus of Nazareth embodies the divine.

## Opening Prayer

*Creator God, who spoke light into darkness and order out of disorder: may your Spirit hover over us as we study the Gospel of John. Illuminate our reading, our hearing, our reflection, and our conversation, that your servant John's ancient words may become for us, by grace, fresh, surprising, challenging, and sustaining words that make us always more ready to receive your Word made flesh, Jesus Christ. Amen.*

## Watch Session Video

Watch the session 1 video segment together. Discuss:

- Which of AJ's statements most interested, intrigued, surprised, or confused you? Why?
- What questions does this video segment raise for you?

# Book Discussion Questions

## *The Fourth Gospel's "Big Bang"*

Invite participants to read John 1:1-5, 14 aloud in unison, from the same translation. (If time allows, read John's entire Prologue, 1:1-18.) Ask participants to speak briefly about the word or phrase from these verses that most catches their attention, and why.

Discuss:

- AJ says the Prologue is John's "version of the big bang." What does she mean, and do you agree? Why or why not?
- "Ancient Israel was an aural rather than visual culture," hearing rather than picturing its stories. To what extent do speaking and hearing create and re-create communal life in your culture? In your family? In your congregation? How, if at all, do you encounter God in what you hear or have heard?
- What claims does John make about "the Word" (*Logos* in Greek) in his Prologue? How do these claims connect to or evoke claims about God's creative activity in Genesis 1 and Proverbs 8:22-36?
- As AJ explains, first-century Stoic philosophy referred to the world's order as *logos*. Do you tend to see more order or disorder in the created world? Why? What examples of order in nature do or might draw your attention to "the Word" John describes?
- "The Word" is, for John, also "the light" (vv. 4-5; see also 1:7-9; 8:12). "The Bible," AJ remarks, "is replete with images of light and dark." Which ones flash most quickly to mind for you? Which have you found most meaningful, and why? What does John mean by identifying "the Word" with "the light"?
- AJ calls readers' attention to one of the four "Servant Songs" in Isaiah. Read Isaiah 42:1-9. How does this passage

connect God's commissioning of the servant to God's creative work? How, specifically, is the servant to be "a light to the nations" (v. 6)? Who else, if anyone, might we identify as the servant?

## The Wedding at Cana

Invite participants to speak briefly about the most memorable wedding reception they've ever attended. What made it so memorable?

Recruit volunteers to read aloud John 2:1-11, taking the roles of the narrator, Jesus, his mother, and "the person in charge" ("the catering manager," AJ).

Discuss:

- AJ suggests seven reasons John could have included the story of Jesus's miracle at Cana as "the first of his signs" (v. 11)—eight, including the suggestion John did so to indicate Jesus's approval of marriage. Which do you find most convincing or compelling, and why? What others, if any, would you suggest?
- AJ says "the third day is the day when miracles occur," citing Genesis 22:4; Exodus 19:11; Hosea 6:2; and the tradition of Jesus's resurrection (e.g., 1 Corinthians 15:4). Is there a day in your life you could point to as a "third day"? What happened to make it so?
- Israel's Scriptures often present God as Israel's bridegroom and husband. Using a print or online concordance, locate and read some of these Old Testament passages. How do they inform your understanding of similar imagery for God and the church in such New Testament passages as 2 Corinthians 11:1-2, or God and the new creation in Revelation 21:2? How does this tradition inform Christian identification of Jesus as a bridegroom, as in John 3:25-30?
- The wedding feast also evokes Israel's understanding of the messianic age as a banquet, as in Isaiah 25:6-9. How does

such imagery increase your understanding and appreciation of the story about wine at a feast in John 2?

- As AJ notes, weddings create new families. How does the wedding at Cana signal the beginning of Jesus's new family? How does John's interest in Jesus's new family shape the way he presents Jesus's mother, in both this story and John 19:25-27?

- Why does Jesus initially respond to his mother's "indirect request" as he does? Is he being rude, as AJ states (and illustrates from Scripture)? Why do you think his mother nevertheless instructs the servants to do what Jesus tells them?

- AJ suggests Jesus's addressing his mother as "woman" underscores "the role that women play in [John's] Gospel." Compare John 2:4 with 4:21 and 20:13. How does each of the women Jesus addresses as "Woman" play an important role in the Gospel?

- What is Jesus's "hour" in John's Gospel (see also 4:21-23; 5:25-29; 7:30; 8:20; 12:23-27; 13:1; 16:21-22, 31-32; 17:1)? How is Jesus's "hour" an example of *kairos* time— opportune and momentous time?

- What times in your life have proven to be kairos times? Did you recognize them as such in the moment? What, if anything, can we do to make ourselves more attuned to *kairos* times when they arrive? How can we recognize potential *kairos* time in the midst of everyday, mundane *chronos* time?

- AJ points out John calls the servants at Cana *diakonoi*, deacons, and "would have known of the church office" by that name. See also 12:26, the term's only other occurrence in John. Taken together, what does the Fourth Gospel suggest about deacons? If your tradition or congregation includes the office of deacons, how does your understanding of it align with John's use of the word?

- Of the servants, AJ wonders, "Are they merely following orders, or do they have 'faith'? Do they realize the import of what is about to happen, and of their role in it?" What do you imagine, and why? To what extent is the servants' faith or absence of faith important in understanding this story? What significance, if any, do you find in the fact that the servants know the source of the wine while their manager does not (v. 9)?

- John says Jesus's disciples "believed in" Jesus as a result of this miracle. AJ asks what, exactly, they believed. What do you think?

- AJ stresses that Jesus's transformation of water to wine is not simply a miracle, but a *sign*—one of seven in John's Gospel, each with a symbolic meaning larger than itself. How would you summarize the larger symbolic meaning of this first of Jesus's signs?

## Closing Your Session

Jesus "revealed his glory" at Cana (2:11) by changing water into wine—arguably, "changing what is to something that is better," which is how AJ describes what it means "to shine as light.... [to be] like God in the act of creation." Read aloud from AJ's book her retelling of the story of Rabbi Israel Salanter and the shoemaker: "As long as the candle is burning, it is still possible to mend."

Lead participants in brainstorming specific, concrete ways your congregation is or could be "changing what is to something that is better." Whom could you be or are helping in these ways? What resources do you have, or what resources could you obtain, to "mend" even more? Write their responses on the newsprint or markerboard. Don't close your session until your group has agreed on at least one practical next step to "shine as light" in your community and the world.

## Closing Prayer

*Jesus our teacher, at Cana you revealed your glory, the glory of the Father's only Son, by increasing joy and providing blessing in abundance. Send us out in your Spirit's strength to reflect your light, doing the works of the One who sent you while it is still day, every day and every hour, until the last. Amen.*

## Optional Extensions

- Discuss how the claims in John's Prologue about creation and the Word's incarnation shape you and your congregation's attitudes toward and involvement in the natural, physical world. How does or how could your congregation work to affirm the created world's goodness and work for its healing?
- Read Wisdom of Solomon 9 (found in Bibles containing the Apocrypha or "deuterocanonical" books). How do John's claims for "the Word" echo this chapter's claims for Wisdom?
- Begin talking with your congregation's leadership about making weddings during the main worship service an option available to couples wanting to get married in your building, or making the practice a congregational norm. How would the congregation be educated about and discuss together reasons for this approach? What liturgical, musical, physical, and scheduling changes might be needed to facilitate it?

# SESSION 2

# Nicodemus and the Samaritan Woman at the Well

## (John 3 & 4)

### Session Goals

This session's reading, reflection, discussion, and prayer will help participants:

- appreciate how wordplay in John 3 and 4 urges both characters and readers to deeper understandings of who Jesus is;
- identify ways in which John's Jesus uses stories from Israel's past to define his meaning and mission;
- remember ordinary moments of blessing and revelation in their own lives; and
- name before God people who are physically, emotionally, and spiritually thirsty, and to consider ways they might bear God's blessing to these individuals.

### Biblical Foundations

*Now there was a Pharisee named Nicodemus, a leader of the Jews. He came to Jesus by night and said to him, "Rabbi, we know that you are a teacher who has come from God, for no one can do these signs that you do unless God is with that person." Jesus answered him, "Very truly, I tell you, no one can see the kingdom of God without being born from above." Nicodemus said to him, "How can anyone be born after having grown old? Can one enter a second time into the mother's womb and be born?" Jesus answered, "Very truly, I tell you, no one can enter the kingdom of God without being born of water and Spirit. What is born of the flesh is flesh, and what is born of the Spirit is spirit. Do not be astonished that I said to you, 'You must be born from above.' The wind blows where it chooses, and you hear the sound of it, but you do not know where it comes from or where it goes. So it is with everyone who is born of the Spirit." Nicodemus said to him, "How can these things be?" Jesus answered him, "Are you the teacher of Israel, and yet you do not understand these things?*

*"Very truly, I tell you, we speak of what we know and testify to what we have seen, yet you do not receive our testimony. If I have told you about earthly things and you do not believe, how can you believe if I tell you about heavenly things? No one has ascended into heaven except the one who descended from heaven, the Son of Man. And just as Moses lifted up the serpent in the wilderness, so must the Son of Man be lifted up, that whoever believes in him may have eternal life."*

*John 3:1-15*

*Now when Jesus learned that the Pharisees had heard, "Jesus is making and baptizing more disciples than John" (although it was not Jesus himself but his disciples who baptized), he left Judea and started back to Galilee. But he had to go through Samaria. So he came to a Samaritan city called Sychar, near the plot of ground that Jacob had given to his son Joseph. Jacob's well was there, and Jesus, tired out by his journey, was sitting by the well. It was about noon.*

*A Samaritan woman came to draw water, and Jesus said to her, "Give me a drink." (His disciples had gone to the city to buy food.) The Samaritan woman said to him, "How is it that you, a Jew, ask a drink of me, a woman of Samaria?" (Jews do not share things in common with Samaritans.) Jesus answered her, "If you knew the gift of God and who it is that is saying to you, 'Give me a drink,' you would have asked him, and he would have given you living water." The woman said to him, "Sir, you have no bucket, and the well is deep. Where do you get that living water? Are you greater than our ancestor Jacob, who gave us the well and with his sons and his flocks drank from it?" Jesus said to her, "Everyone who drinks of this water will be thirsty again, but those who drink of the water that I will give them will never be thirsty. The water that I will give will become in them a spring of water gushing up to eternal life." The woman said to him, "Sir, give me this water, so that I may never be thirsty or have to keep coming here to draw water."*

*Jesus said to her, "Go, call your husband, and come back." The woman answered him, "I have no husband." Jesus said to her, "You are right in saying, 'I have no husband,' for you have had five husbands, and the one you have now is not your husband. What you have said is true!" The woman said to him, "Sir, I see that you are a prophet. Our ancestors worshiped on this mountain, but you say that the place where people must worship is in Jerusalem." Jesus said to her, "Woman, believe me, the hour is coming when you will worship the Father neither on this mountain nor in Jerusalem. You worship what you do not know; we worship what we know, for salvation is from the Jews. But the hour is coming and is now here when the true worshipers will worship the Father in spirit and truth, for the Father seeks such as these to worship him. God is spirit, and those who worship him must worship in spirit and truth." The woman said to him, "I know that Messiah is coming" (who is called Christ). "When he comes, he will proclaim all things to us." Jesus said to her, "I am he, the one who is speaking to you."*

*Just then his disciples came. They were astonished that he was speaking with a woman, but no one said, "What do you want?" or "Why are you speaking with her?" Then the woman left her water jar and went back to the city. She said to the people, "Come and see a man who told me everything I have ever done! He cannot be the Messiah, can he?" They left the city and were on their way to him.*

*John 4:1-30*

## Before Your Session

- Carefully and prayerfully read this session's Biblical Foundations, more than once. Note words and phrases that attract your attention and meditate on them. Write down questions you have, and try to answer them, consulting trusted Bible commentaries. Become as familiar with these Scriptures as possible.

- Carefully read the introduction and chapter 2 of AJ's book more than once.
- You will need: either Bibles for in-person participants or screen slides prepared with Scripture texts for sharing (identify the translation used), or both; newsprint or a markerboard and markers (for in-person sessions).
- If using the DVD or streaming video, preview the session 2 video segment. Choose the best time in your session plan for viewing it.
- Consider whether you want to form two groups of participants for this session, assigning one group to study John 3 and the other John 4, each reporting to the other before the session ends; or whether you will study both stories with the whole group.
- Water and cups for each participant.

## Starting Your Session

Welcome participants. Invite volunteers to tell the best puns they know. Be ready to start the joke-swapping with a pun of your own. (Please keep your puns clean enough for your group's comfort level!)

Tell participants the stories from John in this session also involve some wordplay—puns, double (even triple) meanings, and even flirty innuendo. As AJ notes, these stories show us how understanding Jesus "requires not only rational thought but also divine revelation." In both, Jesus, the Word made flesh, "takes vocabulary, words, out of their mundane, fleshy meaning and moves them toward the transcendent."

## Opening Prayer

*Holy God, whose word will stand forever: your Spirit blows where your Spirit wills, yet we dare to ask you send your wind to sweep over our study, that we may read, hear, and live the words of him who declares all things, Jesus the Messiah. Amen.*

## Watch Session Video

Watch the session 2 video segment together. Discuss:

- Which of AJ's statements most interested, intrigued, surprised, or confused you? Why?
- What questions does this video segment raise for you?

## Book Discussion Questions

### Nicodemus "In the Dark"

Recruit volunteers to read aloud John 3:1-15, taking the roles of the narrator, Jesus, and Nicodemus. Discuss:

- AJ appreciates Nicodemus's "willingness to pursue what he finds interesting and important," but finds his nighttime and stealthy approach problematic. Is your opinion of Nicodemus mostly favorable, mostly unfavorable, or mixed? Why? When was a time you showed the courage to admit you didn't know something and sought answers?
- Why does AJ say the usual English translation of "Amen, Amen..." as "very truly..." (vv. 3, 5, 11) is inadequate? When can you remember starting a conversation with wishes and hopes regarding its outcome? What wishes and hopes, if any, do you imagine Jesus has for Nicodemus as they begin this conversation?
- As AJ notes, John explicitly mentions "the kingdom of God" only twice (vv. 3, 5), and may expect readers to bring what they know about God's kingdom from the Synoptic Gospels (Matthew, Mark, and Luke) to his Gospel. How do you define, explain, or think about the kingdom of God?
- Jesus tells Nicodemus none can see God's kingdom without being born *anōthen*, which can mean "above, anew, and again," and also "from the top" or "from the beginning." Why does AJ say "born again," arguably the most familiar

21

English rendering, is "not a good translation" of the phrase? How does holding the word's multiple meanings in mind at once shape your understanding of what Jesus is saying?

- Jesus's references to "water" and "spirit" (v. 5) may evoke Christian baptism for John's readers, in the first century and today. How do your congregation's baptismal practices present baptism as a kind of "birth from above"?

- AJ refers to friends and students who have described their baptisms as "transcendent moment[s] ... in their lives when confusion gives way to clarity, or, to draw from [John's] Prologue, when chaos yields to order." When, if ever, have you experienced such moments yourself? To what extent were they a "birth from above" for you, and how do they continue to affect and shape you?

- The Greek word *pneuma (NOO-ma)* means "wind," "spirit," and "breath." How do these multiple, simultaneous meanings help you understand Jesus's words in verse 8? How do they shape your understanding and experience of the Holy Spirit?

- Read the "weird account" of the serpent Moses lifted up in the wilderness in Numbers 21:4-9. How does this story illustrate Jesus's meaning and purpose for John? Does the story help you understand more about Jesus? Why or why not?

- AJ states that, for John, "eternal life" "does not mean 'live forever and not die.'" What does eternal life mean? When does eternal life begin? (See also 6:47, 54; 11:25-26; 17:1-3.)

- AJ remarks that readers who understand the puns Nicodemus finds so confusing may feel superior to Nicodemus. How can readers appreciate John letting them "in on the secret" without feeling "special" or smug about it? Why is it important for Christians to avoid elitism when interpreting Jesus's words—not only in John 3 but anywhere in Scripture?

- Nicodemus appears twice more in John, at 7:50-51 and 19:39-42. AJ concludes Nicodemus "remains in the dark" by the Gospel's end. Do you agree? Why or why not?

## Words with a Woman at a Well

Recruit volunteers to read aloud John 4:1-30 (through v. 42 if time allows), taking the roles of the narrator, Jesus, the woman, and Jesus's disciples (and the Samaritans, v. 42). Discuss:

- Read 2 Chronicles 28:8-15; 2 Kings 17:21-24; and Nehemiah 4:1-8. How do these stories of tension and conflict between Judah (the ancient Southern Kingdom, with its capital in Jerusalem) and Israel (the ancient Northern Kingdom, with its capital in Samaria) set the stage for the gap between Jews and Samaritans in Jesus's day (v. 9)?
- Geographically speaking, as AJ notes, Jesus would not have "had to go through Samaria" (v. 4) to go from Judea to Galilee. What is the "theological necessity" of his journey through Samaria?
- How does this story's midday setting reinforce John's use of light and dark imagery (for example, contrast John 3:2; 9:4; 13:27-30)?
- Read Genesis 24:10-20; 29:1-11; Exodus 2:15b-21. What expectations might these biblical stories of men and women meeting at wells create for readers of John 4? How does John 4 interact with those expectations?
- For AJ, Jesus and the woman's conversation is a model of how "[d]ifferences can be maintained, strongly, and at the same time friendship can flower." When have you found friendship with someone despite strong differences? How can people intentionally cultivate such friendships? What does or might your congregation do to encourage such friendships?

- When has water been, as AJ says, "so much more" to you than "colorless, tasteless liquid"? What does the image of "living water" ("running water") bring to your mind? When and why is it preferable to still water?

- How does the prophet Jeremiah use the image of "living water" (2:12-13; 17:13)? What makes Jeremiah's usage significant for John 4?

- What do you think of AJ's suggestion that the woman engages in "sexual banter" with Jesus at the well (v. 11)? (See Proverbs 5:15-18; Song of Songs 4:12-15.) Do you think Jesus was embarrassed about or offended by sexual innuendo? Why or why not?

- How does the woman's mention of Jacob (v. 12) undermine the earlier claim that Jews and Samaritans have nothing in common (v. 9)? How does Jesus and the woman's conversation challenge it? How do you seek out what you may have in common with others who are different from you? How does your congregation?

- AJ notes how frequently commentators see the woman at the well in Samaria as "variously, a gold digger, an impossible wife, or a slut." What other reasons for her several past marriages are possible?

- Referring to the woman's eventual realization of who Jesus is, AJ writes, "Revelation need not come all at once; it can proceed in steps, and so it can grow." How have you experienced the gradual growth of revelation in your life?

- How does the woman's invitation to her fellow Samaritans echo the invitations Jesus extends in 1:39 and Philip extends in 1:46? How do or could you and your congregation follow this invitational model of evangelism?

## Closing Your Session

Read aloud from AJ's book: "I wonder how our lives would change if with each glass of water... we thought about people who thirst, or Jesus who thirsts. Every swallow becomes a blessing. When that occurs, we are feeling the effects... of living water."

Pour a cup of water for each participant. (Those participating virtually will need to get their own cup of water.) Invite participants to take a drink of water and think about an ordinary moment in their life they have or could look back on as a moment of blessing or revelation. Invite those who wish to share aloud to briefly do so.

Invite participants to take another drink of water and think about someone they know or know of who is physically, emotionally, or spiritually thirsting. Invite volunteers to talk briefly about what they are doing or could do to serve that person; and to name that person, aloud or silently, during the Closing Prayer.

## Closing Prayer

*Jesus, you are living water for all who thirst. Quench the thirsting bodies and souls of those we name before you, aloud or in our hearts: [pause for names]. Refresh us, too, that as we invite others to come and see how fully you know and love them, we may go and show your love in our lives, bearing your blessing to them. Amen.*

## Optional Extensions

- Research Nicodemus and the Samaritan woman as saints in the Eastern Orthodox tradition. What can you find individual Eastern Orthodox Christians saying about why they revere them? How, if at all, do their histories as saints in Eastern Orthodoxy cast new light on their stories in John?
- AJ notes Jesus's words in chapter 4, verse 26 are the first of his "I am" statements in John. Most of these statements

are poetic metaphors, since "[n]o words can fully express divinity." Look up and read the rest of the "I am" statements in John, referring to either AJ's book or a biblical concordance or commentary, or both. Which of these statements appeal most to you, and why?

- Research and choose a trustworthy charitable organization or ministry dedicated to giving people access to clean water for your group to financially support together.

# SESSION 3

# The Healing of the Man at the Pool

## (John 5)

### Session Goals

This session's reading, reflection, discussion, and prayer will help participants:

- read and appreciate John's account of Jesus healing a man at Bethesda as both a healing story and a controversy story,
- reflect on whether and how they keep Sabbath, and
- identify people who are ill and caregivers for people who are ill whom they and their congregation can help and support.

### Biblical Foundation

*After this there was a festival of the Jews, and Jesus went up to Jerusalem.*

*Now in Jerusalem by the Sheep Gate there is a pool, called in Hebrew Beth-zatha, which has five porticoes. In these lay many ill, blind, lame, and paralyzed people. One man was there who had been ill for thirty-eight years. When Jesus saw him lying there and knew that he had been there a long time, he said to him, "Do you want to be made well?" The ill man answered him, "Sir, I have no one to put me into the pool when the water is stirred up, and while I am making my way someone else steps down ahead of me." Jesus said to him, "Stand up, take your mat and walk." At once the man was made well, and he took up his mat and began to walk.*

*Now that day was a Sabbath. So the Jews said to the man who had been cured, "It is the Sabbath; it is not lawful for you to carry your mat." But he answered them, "The man who made me well said to me, 'Take up your mat and walk.'" They asked him, "Who is the man who said to you, 'Take it up and walk'?" Now the man who had been healed did not know who it was, for Jesus had disappeared in the crowd that was there. Later Jesus found him in the temple and said to him, "See, you have been made well! Do not sin any more, so that nothing worse happens to you." The man went away and told the Jews that it was Jesus who had made him well. Therefore the Jews started persecuting Jesus, because he was doing such things on the Sabbath.*

*John 5:1-16*

## Before Your Session

- Carefully and prayerfully read this session's Biblical Foundation, more than once. Note words and phrases that attract your attention, and meditate on them. Write down questions you have, and try to answer them, consulting trusted Bible commentaries. Become as familiar with these Scriptures as possible.
- Carefully read the introduction and chapter 3 of AJ's book more than once.
- You will need: either Bibles for in-person participants or screen slides prepared with Scripture texts for sharing (identify the translation used), or both; newsprint or a markerboard and markers (for in-person sessions).
- If using the DVD or streaming video, preview the session 3 video segment. Choose the best time in your session plan for viewing it.

## Starting Your Session

Welcome participants. Invite them to either remember whatever they can about their own lives or the larger world thirty-eight years prior to your session, or both. (For example, if you're conducting your session in 2024, ask them to think back to 1986.) Were they alive? Where did they live? What music were they listening to? What books where they reading? What films and TV shows were they watching? What were the biggest events for their family, their community, the nation, and the world that year? (If your preparation time allows, you may want to find music from that year and have it playing in your in-person meeting space as participants gather, to help jog memories!)

Read aloud from AJ's book: in Scripture, thirty-eight years "can function as an approximation of the passing of a generation (the typical count for a generation is forty years)." Ask participants to imagine being sick for thirty-eight years—nearly an entire generation. (Do not assume imagining such a long-term illness will be difficult for everyone.) Tell them the story from John in this session introduces Jesus and us to a man who has been ill for thirty-eight years.

## Opening Prayer

*Living God, you desire wholeness for all, and your Spirit is always at work for well-being. Stir up our minds and hearts as we again study the Scriptures, that we may see and know who it is that calls us to walk in his ways, our Lord Jesus Christ. Amen.*

## Watch Session Video

Watch the session 3 video segment together. Discuss:

- Which of AJ's statements most interested, intrigued, surprised, or confused you? Why?
- What questions does this video segment raise for you?

# Book Discussion Questions

## *John 5: A Healing Story*

Recruit volunteers to read aloud John 5:1-9a (through "and began to walk"), taking the roles of the narrator, Jesus, and the man who is ill. Discuss:

- John says this story takes place during "a festival of the Jews," but does not specify which of the three pilgrim festivals: Passover, Shavuot, or Sukkot. Why not? Which do each of these festivals celebrate? (See Exodus 12:26-27 for Passover; Leviticus 23:15-22 for Shavuot [Weeks], although Shavuot also became a celebration of God's gift of the Torah; and Leviticus 23:39-43 for Sukkot [Booths].) How might each one be an appropriate setting for the story John tells?

- "Too often," AJ observes, "I find that church programs, with few exceptions, are not celebratory." Do you agree? Why or why not? What changes would you make—and how could you start making them?

- AJ remarks this story raises questions of "who 'celebrates' and how best can one celebrate if one cannot participate in all the activities." How accessible are your congregation's physical space and your regular worship activities to people with physical challenges and disabilities? What changes will your congregation make to become more accessible?

- AJ suggests the Aramaic name "Beth-zatha" (v. 2) may mean "something like 'house of grace' or 'house of divine steadfastness,'" and would thus be "an appropriate name for a place known for healing." How so? Where are some places, if any, you have especially experienced God's grace or steadfastness?

- Does your Bible include verse 4 in the text, as a footnote, or at all? Do you find the verse as "troubling" as AJ finds it? Why or why not?

- The man by the pool has been ill for thirty-eight years, a number AJ, following Cyril of Alexandria, suggests may evoke Deuteronomy 2:14: "the time for one ethos, that of enslavement and the battles to counter its effects, to be replaced by another, that of freedom and the concerns for what one can do now and in the future." How might reflecting on the transition from the Exodus generation of Israelites to the next generation shape your understanding of this healing story?

- Why doesn't John specify the man's illness (v. 5)?

- AJ has concluded Jesus's question to the man, "Do you want to be made healthy?" is a "profound" one. Do you agree? Have you ever known someone who is ill who didn't want to be well? Have you ever been sick and not wanted to be well? Why or why not?

- AJ characterizes the man's response to Jesus's question as one "designed to evoke pity." What are some other possible ways to make sense of his response (for example, AJ also allows the man could be "exhausted")? Which interpretation(s) do you find most convincing and why?

- How does the image of the pool's stirred-up water (v. 7) connect this story to the "living water" about which Jesus spoke to the woman at the well in John 4?

- AJ criticizes the man's lack of response to the healing Jesus performs. Do you join her criticism of him? Why or why not?

### John 5: A Controversy Story

Recruit volunteers to read aloud John 5:9b ("Now that day was a Sabbath"), taking the roles of the narrator, Jesus, the cured man, and "the Jews" (v. 10). Tell participants, as AJ notes, that John here turns a healing story into a "controversy story"—a story about disagreements between Jesus and those who oppose his teachings or actions. Discuss:

- John uses the phrase "the Jews" some seventy times in his Gospel, almost always as a derogatory reference to Jesus's opponents. Why must readers today distinguish John's specific usage from all Jewish people in the first century? from all Jewish people of any time and any place?

- How does imagining whether the Jewish leaders recognized the man who had been healed or witnessed the healing (v. 12 suggests they did not) affect how we understand their statement in verse 10?

- "Jesus had not only raised [the man] up," states AJ; "he has set him up." Do you agree? Why or why not?

- Do you interpret the man's response in verse 11 as a failure to take responsibility, as AJ does? Why or why not?

- AJ suggests the man could have responded in several other ways. Which of her various proposed responses do you prefer? Can you think of other things the man might or should have said?

- As AJ notes, attention to what does or doesn't count as "work" on the Sabbath continues to be a vital issue for many Jewish people, especially Orthodox Jews, as well as among many Christians. What are the theological reasons for Sabbath observance? (See Exodus 20:8-11; Deuteronomy 5:12-15; Jeremiah 17:19-22.) Whether your Sabbath is Saturday, Sunday, or some other day, how do you and your congregation keep it holy—and how seriously do you do so?

- AJ finds the idea of "not carrying" helpful. How do you determine what you can and cannot, should and should not, carry with you on a daily basis? On the Sabbath day? How do these questions apply to the intangible things we "carry" with us through our days?

- According to AJ, what Jesus tells the man in verse 14 suggests the man's long illness had been due to his own sin. Do you read Jesus's words the same way? Why or why not?
- Do you believe sin and sickness or disability are ever connected? Always connected? Never connected? How do beliefs about sin and sickness influence the way we attend to and value (or fail to) health care for ourselves and others?
- What could be the "something worse" than thirty-eight years of sickness against which Jesus warns the man? AJ suspects it may be "eternal damnation," since John's Gospel has a stark, "binary view" of salvation and damnation (see, for example, 3:16-18, 31-36; 5:24-29). What do you think?
- AJ compares belief to love—"a matter of the heart, not the intellect." What roles do you think the heart and the intellect play in faith, and why?
- In telling the Jewish leaders about Jesus (v. 15), the man "had to have known that he was setting Jesus up," states AJ. Do you agree? Why or why not?

## Closing Your Session

The man by the pool told Jesus he had no one to help him get into the water when it was stirred up (v. 7). "And yet," notes AJ, "he is still alive, which means that someone has provided him food, [and] helped him with cleaning up after basic bodily functions. Perhaps he leaves the pool in the evening to return to a home where there are people to help him."

Tell participants that while we don't have all the details of the man's situation, we may know the situations of people in poor health whom we can help. We may also know caregivers whom we can support. Discuss:

- When have you acted as a caregiver for someone who is or was ill?

- How were you or how would you like to have been supported by others when acting as that caregiver?
- What is your congregation doing or could it do to increase the access people who are ill have to health care?

## Closing Prayer

*Jesus, we want to be well, in body, mind, and spirit. We praise you for your life-giving presence and power. We confess we do not always take the actions or the responsibility we could to nurture well-being in ourselves and in others. Heal us of any resistance to your Spirit's movement in and around us, that we may live as the whole people and community God created us to be. Amen.*

## Optional Extensions

- AJ briefly compares and contrasts John 5:1-16 with Mark 2:1-12. Do the same, and discuss how the stories help interpret each other.
- Research what archaeologists know about the site of this healing story. How, if at all, does this information affect your understanding of the story?
- "I still wonder about all those other people waiting by the pool," writes AJ. "What might they be thinking?" Try telling the story in John 5 from one of these onlookers' perspectives. What new insights into the story does telling it from a new point of view yield?
- Talk with a religiously observant Jewish person about how and why they observe Sabbath, and what their observance means to them. Remember you are seeking information and conversation—not a religious controversy of your own.

# SESSION 4

# The Man Born Blind

## (John 9)

### Session Goals

This session's reading, reflection, discussion, and prayer will help participants:

- think in a critical, nuanced way about how John uses imagery of light and darkness;
- engage in a close reading of John 9, paying special attention to its symbolism and its relationship to other Scriptures; and
- consider how the depiction of faith in John 9 informs the way they and their congregation witness to Jesus.

### Biblical Foundation

*As [Jesus] walked along, he saw a man blind from birth. His disciples asked him, "Rabbi, who sinned, this man or his parents, that he was born blind?" Jesus answered, "Neither this man nor his parents sinned; he was born blind so that God's works might be revealed in him. We must work the works of him who sent me while it is day; night is coming, when no one can work. As long as I am in the world, I am the light of the world." When he had said this, he spat on the ground and made mud with the saliva and spread the mud on the man's eyes, saying to him, "Go, wash in the pool of Siloam" (which means Sent). Then he went and washed and came back able to see. The neighbors and those who had seen him before as a beggar began to ask, "Is this not the man who used to sit and beg?" Some were saying, "It is he." Others were saying, "No, but it is someone like him." He kept saying, "I am he." But they kept asking him, "Then how were your eyes opened?" He answered, "The man called Jesus made mud, spread it on my eyes, and said to me, 'Go to Siloam and wash.' Then I went and washed and received my sight." They said to him, "Where is he?" He said, "I do not know."*

*They brought to the Pharisees the man who had formerly been blind. Now it was a Sabbath day when Jesus made the mud and opened his eyes. Then the Pharisees also began to ask him how he had received his sight. He said to them, "He put mud on my eyes. Then I washed, and now I see." Some of the Pharisees said, "This man is not from God, for he does not observe the Sabbath." Others said, "How can a man who is a sinner perform such signs?" And they were divided. So they said again to the blind man, "What do you say about him? It was your eyes he opened." He said, "He is a prophet."*

*The Jews did not believe that he had been blind and had received his sight until they called the parents of the man who had received his sight and asked them, "Is this your son, who you say was born blind? How then does he now see?" His parents answered, "We know that this is our son and that he was born blind, but we do not know how it is that now he sees, nor do we know who opened his eyes. Ask him; he is of age. He will speak for himself." His parents said this because they were afraid of the Jews, for the Jews had already agreed that anyone who confessed Jesus to be the Messiah would be put out of the synagogue. Therefore his parents said, "He is of age; ask him."*

*So for the second time they called the man who had been blind, and they said to him, "Give glory to God! We know that this man is a sinner." He answered, "I do not know whether he is a sinner. One thing I do know, that though I was blind, now I see." They said to him, "What did he do to you? How did he open your eyes?" He answered them, "I have told you already, and you would not listen. Why do you want to hear it again? Do you also want to become his disciples?" Then they reviled him, saying, "You are his disciple, but we are disciples of Moses. We know that God has spoken to Moses, but as for this man, we do not know where he comes from." The man answered, "Here is an astonishing thing! You do not know where he comes from, yet he opened my eyes. We know that God does not listen to sinners, but he does listen to one who worships him and obeys his will. Never since the world began has it been heard that anyone opened the eyes of a person born blind. If this man were not from God, he could do nothing." They answered him, "You were born entirely in sins, and are you trying to teach us?" And they drove him out.*

*Jesus heard that they had driven him out, and when he found him he said, "Do you believe in the Son of Man?" He answered, "And who is he, sir? Tell me, so that I may believe in him." Jesus said to him, "You have seen him, and the one speaking with you is he." He said, "Lord, I believe." And he worshiped him. Jesus said, "I came into this world for judgment, so that those who do not see may see and those who do see may become blind." Some of the Pharisees who were with him heard this and said to him, "Surely we are not blind, are we?" Jesus said to them, "If you were blind, you would not have sin. But now that you say, 'We see,' your sin remains."*

*John 9:1-41*

## Before Your Session

- Carefully and prayerfully read this session's Biblical Foundation more than once. Note words and phrases that attract your attention, and meditate on them. Write down questions you have, and try to answer them, consulting trusted Bible commentaries. Become as familiar with these Scriptures as possible.
- Carefully read the introduction and chapter 4 of AJ's book more than once.
- You will need: either Bibles for in-person participants or screen slides prepared with Scripture texts for sharing (identify the translation used), or both; newsprint or a markerboard and markers (for in-person sessions).

- If using the DVD or streaming video, preview the session 4 video segment. Choose the best time in your session plan for viewing it.

## Starting Your Session

Welcome participants. Invite your group to sing (or read aloud) together the first verse of "Amazing Grace." (Either print and distribute the words or put them on a slide for sharing, or both, if needed; https://hymnary.org/text/amazing_grace_how_sweet_the_sound.) Ask:

- What does the metaphor "was blind, but now I see" mean in this hymn? What does it mean to you personally?
- How is imagery of physical blindness and sight helpful for discussing spiritual conditions? How is it limited, as all metaphorical images are limited? What other imagery, if any, might you use to convey similar meanings?
- AJ notes the Gospels' connection of "physical blindness with moral dimness . . . shows the privilege, and the ignorance, of sighted people." How so? How should this recognition inform the use of such imagery in faith communities today?
- Read Genesis 1:1-2; Deuteronomy 5:22-23; and 1 Kings 8:12, all verses AJ cites to point out how darkness can also be revelatory. How does this biblical dimension of darkness shape your attitude toward the dark? What truths about yourself, other people, or God, if any, have you discovered in darkness?

Encourage participants to keep this discussion in mind as, in this session, your group explores the story in John 9 of Jesus giving sight to a man born blind.

## Opening Prayer

*Holy God, though you dwell in unapproachable light, we are bold to approach you in study and prayer because, in Jesus, you have approached us. May your illuminating Spirit shine on us in this time together, that the eyes of our hearts may see you more clearly, and that we may more faithfully glorify you. Amen.*

## Watch Session Video

Watch the session 4 video segment together. Discuss:

- Which of AJ's statements most interested, intrigued, surprised, or confused you? Why?
- What questions does this video segment raise for you?

## Book Discussion Questions

### Discussing John 9

Recruit volunteers to read John 9 aloud, taking the roles of the narrator, Jesus, Jesus's disciples, the man born blind, his neighbors, his parents, and Pharisees. Discuss:

- What significance, if any, do you find in the fact that this story begins when Jesus sees a man who cannot see him? Who are people you see in your community who don't (or who you think don't) see you? What is keeping you from seeing each other? Which of these barriers to mutual sight could you remove?
- Read Exodus 4:11; Leviticus 19:14; and Deuteronomy 27:18. What do these Scriptures teach about God's relationship to those who are blind, and the place those who are blind have, or ought to have, among God's people?
- Read Ezekiel 18:20 and Jeremiah 31:29-30. How do these Scriptures argue against the disciples' assumption regarding the man's blindness?

- How does Jesus respond to his disciples' assumption about the man? What do you think about his response? Would you, like AJ, have preferred Jesus give them "a lesson on disability"? Why or why not?
- Why does Jesus give the man sight when the man has not asked for it? When should Jesus's followers today emulate this approach? When should they not?
- Why does Jesus use, as AJ says, "hands-on" methods to give the man sight (v. 6)? Why is the man's action required to complete Jesus's miracle (vv. 7-8)? What lessons, if any, can Jesus's followers learn from these circumstances?
- How might the pool of Siloam symbolize new life for the man, as AJ suggests it might?
- The pool's name means "sent." How does this name serve a thematic purpose in this story? in John's Gospel as a whole? (*Optional:* Using a concordance, find some of those "several other 'sent' references reflecting Christology" that AJ mentions.)
- AJ points out that, in John's Greek, the man identifies himself to his neighbors with the words *egō eimi* ("I am," v. 9). Why are these words especially significant in John's Gospel? (Refer to session 2, especially John 4:26; see also 18:5-7.) How do they echo God's revelation to Moses in Exodus 3:13-14? How appropriate or not is the man's use of these words to identify himself at this point, and why?
- Why does John wait until verse 14 to tell readers this story takes place on the Sabbath?
- How do Jesus's actions violate the Sabbath prohibition against work? Why do his actions divide the Pharisees?
- "For John," states AJ, "proclaiming the Gospel can both unite and divide; the same point holds true today." How have you or your congregation experienced this truth for yourselves?

- In verses 18-23, John calls those who interrogate the man's parents "the Jews." AJ states there is "no early evidence of Jews expelling [from synagogues] fellow Jews who proclaimed Jesus to be Lord." What does John want to communicate to his readers with his language about "the Jews"? How can Christians read stories like this today in ways that are not anti-Jewish and anti-Judaism?
- What do you think about the man's parents? When have you been in a situation where you acted, in AJ's words, out of "fear rather than faith"? What did you learn from that situation that has helped or could help you act more faithfully in the future?
- What is the sin of which Jesus judges these Pharisees (vv. 39-41)? When have you encountered people who claim to "see" but who are "blind"? When have you been such a person yourself? How did you realize, and what have you done about it?

## Closing Your Session

Read aloud from AJ's book: "Faith is no more of a choice than is sight.... Condemning people for not believing is not a helpful choice; showing love as manifested in action is." Ask:

- What insights into the nature of faith can we take from the story in John 9?
- How can or do these insights specifically shape the way we witness to Jesus, as individuals and as a congregation? What ought we continue to do? What ought we do differently? Why?

## Closing Prayer

*Lord Jesus, you see us even when we cannot or will not see you. Help us to see where and in whom you are revealing God's works today, that we may worship you and do your will, loving one another and our neighbors as your faithful disciples. Amen.*

## Optional Extensions

- Research what archaeologists know (and don't know) about the pool of Siloam. How, if at all, does this information affect your understanding of the story?
- Research the use of "miqveh" (ritual baths) in ancient and modern Judaism. How does this information affect your understanding of this story?
- Compare and contrast this healing and controversy story with that in John 5 (session 3), as AJ does. How does reading the stories together help you understand each better? What questions about each story does the other one raise?

# SESSION 5

## Foot Washing

## (John 12 & 13)

### Session Goals

This session's reading, reflection, discussion, and prayer will help participants:

- reflect on the Passover context of the stories of Mary anointing Jesus and Jesus washing his disciples' feet,
- appreciate the rich significance of the acts of service in these two stories by considering them from multiple perspectives, and
- make plans for a corporeal act of service the group can perform together.

### Biblical Foundations

*Six days before the Passover Jesus came to Bethany, the home of Lazarus, whom he had raised from the dead. There they gave a dinner for him. Martha served, and Lazarus was one of those reclining with him. Mary took a pound of costly perfume made of pure nard, anointed Jesus's feet, and wiped them with her hair. The house was filled with the fragrance of the perfume. But Judas Iscariot, one of his disciples (the one who was about to betray him), said, "Why was this perfume not sold for three hundred denarii and the money given to the poor?" (He said this not because he cared about the poor but because he was a thief; he kept the common purse and used to steal what was put into it.) Jesus said,*

43

*"Leave her alone. She bought it so that she might keep it for the day of my burial. You always have the poor with you, but you do not always have me."*

*John 12:1-8*

*Now before the festival of the Passover, Jesus knew that his hour had come to depart from this world and go to the Father. Having loved his own who were in the world, he loved them to the end. The devil had already decided that Judas son of Simon Iscariot would betray Jesus. And during supper Jesus, knowing that the Father had given all things into his hands and that he had come from God and was going to God, got up from supper, took off his outer robe, and tied a towel around himself. Then he poured water into a basin and began to wash the disciples' feet and to wipe them with the towel that was tied around him. He came to Simon Peter, who said to him, "Lord, are you going to wash my feet?" Jesus answered, "You do not know now what I am doing, but later you will understand." Peter said to him, "You will never wash my feet." Jesus answered, "Unless I wash you, you have no share with me." Simon Peter said to him, "Lord, not my feet only but also my hands and my head!" Jesus said to him, "One who has bathed does not need to wash, except for the feet, but is entirely clean. And you are clean, though not all of you." For he knew who was to betray him; for this reason he said, "Not all of you are clean."*

*After he had washed their feet, had put on his robe, and had reclined again, he said to them, "Do you know what I have done to you? You call me Teacher and Lord, and you are right, for that is what I am. So if I, your Lord and Teacher, have washed your feet, you also ought to wash one another's feet. For I have set you an example, that you also should do as I have done to you. Very truly, I tell you, slaves are not greater than their master, nor are messengers greater than the one who sent them. If you know these things, you are blessed if you do them."*

*John 13:1-17*

## Before Your Session

- Carefully and prayerfully read this session's Biblical Foundation more than once. Note words and phrases that

attract your attention, and meditate on them. Write down
questions you have, and try to answer them, consulting
trusted Bible commentaries. Become as familiar with these
Scriptures as possible.

- Carefully read the introduction and chapter 5 of AJ's book
  more than once.

- You will need: either Bibles for in-person participants
  or screen slides prepared with Scripture texts for sharing
  (identify the translation used), or both; newsprint or a
  markerboard and markers (for in-person sessions).

- If using the DVD or streaming video, preview the session
  5 video segment. Choose the best time in your session plan
  for viewing it.

## Starting Your Session

Welcome participants. Tell participants the two main stories in
this session take place six days and one day, respectively, before the last
Passover during Jesus's earthly ministry. Ask:

- What does Passover commemorate? (God delivering the
  Israelites from slavery in Egypt, so named because God's
  judgment against the Egyptians "passed over" houses of
  the Israelites, marked with a sacrificial lamb's blood;
  Exodus 12:12-13)
- Have you ever participated in modern Jewish celebrations of
  Passover? What did you see, hear, taste, touch, and smell?
- AJ describes her own family's preparations for Passover.
  How do you "go into overdrive" before a significant holiday?
- Jesus knows this Passover will be his last (indeed, in John,
  he does not get to celebrate the Passover seder, as he does
  in the other Gospels). How would you celebrate the next
  upcoming major holiday, whatever it is, differently if you
  knew it would be your last? How might this thought prompt
  you to change how you celebrate that holiday anyway?

## Opening Prayer

*Liberating God, you saved your people from bondage that they might be free to serve you alone. May our time of study today serve you, that we might more faithfully obey the commandment our Teacher and Lord, Jesus, gave us to love one another, for we worship him as your lamb, slain for our sin and the sin of the world. Amen.*

## Watch Session Video

Watch the session 5 video segment together. Discuss:

- Which of AJ's statements most interested, intrigued, surprised, or confused you? Why?
- What questions does this video segment raise for you?

## Book Discussion Questions

### *Mary Anoints Jesus's Feet*

Recruit volunteers to read aloud John 12:1-8, taking the roles of the narrator, Judas, and Jesus. Discuss:

- What associations does AJ note Bethany has for Jesus and his disciples? Where is a place that holds "traces of the sacred" for you, and why? Where is a "Bethany" to which you might go, or have gone, for a "moment of respite" before a difficult time you knew awaited you?
- John introduces Bethany differently in 11:1 and 12:1, about which AJ observes, "The city takes on new meaning depending on how it is introduced." What places have changed meaning for you over time, and how?
- Who, if anyone, has ever given you a dinner, and for what reason(s)? Do you prefer being the host or a guest at a dinner? Why?

- Although John states that "Martha served" (v. 2), how might we also see Lazarus and Mary serving Jesus at this dinner?
- AJ notes that Lazarus's body "testifies to what Jesus can do." What, if anything, distinguishes these two bodies from each other as capable of showing both mortality and majesty? from any other human body, then or now? How does choosing to see other people's bodies as manifesting mortality and majesty affect the way we treat others? What about seeing our own bodies that way?
- John doesn't state Mary's motivation. AJ says Mary "modeled gratitude." What do you think motivated Mary to anoint and wipe Jesus's feet?
- AJ rejects the common interpretation of Mary's anointing as "transgressive," but states it is "effusive." Do you think we are inclined to view effusive displays of affection as transgressive? Why or why not?
- AJ states Mary's action can bear multiple meanings and associations: a healing touch, a sensual touch, an expression of mourning. Which of these interpretations appeals most strongly to you, and why? What can you appreciate about interpretations that do not appeal as strongly?
- How does Mary's action reveal her "sense of worth, of competence, and of agency," as AJ says it does? How does your congregation encourage people to see themselves as capable of giving service? How much, if at all, does it define people's worth solely in terms of how they can serve others?
- The fragrance of Mary's nard filled the house (v. 3). What fragrances do you associate with love? Why is Judas unable to recognize the scent of Mary's perfume as the scent of love?

- "What is generous to one person," writes AJ, "is a waste to another." When, if ever, have you or your congregation been criticized for "wasting" money for what you believed to be a loving reason? What criteria do you and your congregation use to decide how and where you want to invest?

- Why does Jesus commend Mary's action? How is Mary's action, as AJ suggests, an appropriate recognition that "death will come to us all"? How is it an appropriate recognition of Jesus's death specifically?

### Jesus Washes the Feet of "His Own"

Recruit volunteers to read aloud John 13:1-17, taking the roles of the narrator, Jesus, and Peter. Discuss:

- What is "the hour" Jesus knows has come (v. 1)? Why is it important? AJ writes that, for John, this "hour" is also "whenever anyone makes a decision to follow Jesus, or not." Can you point to such a specific "hour" in your own experience?

- Why does AJ distinguish the love with which Jesus loves his disciples from God's love toward the world (as in John 3:16)? Do you find this distinction helpful or not, and why?

- The word for the "end" to which Jesus loves his disciples, as AJ states, is the Greek word "*telos*," meaning "goal." How would you describe or explain the goal of Jesus's love for "his own"?

- How do you understand the extent to which Judas is responsible for betraying Jesus (vv. 2, 18)? Is Judas among Jesus's "own," whom he loves "to the end"? Why or why not?

- How is Jesus's knowledge of his origin and his destination an important context for this story (v. 3)? When was a time a knowledge of your origins and a sense of your future have helped you "not only to endure but also to grow, to create, and to improve," as AJ states they can?

- Why do you think John describes Jesus's actions in verses 4-5 as slowly and deliberately as he does?

- AJ writes, "I think I would find it more difficult to show such vulnerability and servitude in front of people who looked up to me or depended on me…than before strangers." When was a time you found it difficult to be vulnerable before or to serve someone you know well, and who knows you well?

- Why is Simon Peter's response to Jesus's action (v. 6) "a very good question"? As AJ notes, John never revisits this scene, leaving us to decide what Peter will understand about it "later" (v. 7). What do you think Jesus is referring to, and why?

- Foot washing was a common, everyday act in Jesus's society. What actions in society today, if any, represent the kind of subordinate service Jesus enacts, and which he calls his disciples to emulate?

- "Those who have their feet washed by disciples are to feel worthy," writes AJ, and "to feel themselves recognized as children of God." When has someone served you in a way that made you feel seen as a child of God? How do you and your congregation strive to serve others in that way?

- Jesus's commandment to love each other (13:34) is not new (Leviticus 19:18), writes AJ; what is new is the commandment to love as Jesus has loved (see John 15:12-13). Who do you know or know about who has died for another out of love? Is it possible to love others as Jesus loved without dying? Why or why not?

- "Jesus does for Peter," writes AJ, "in effect what Mary did for him." When has someone's act of generous, costly service to you inspired you to perform a similar act of service for someone else?

## Closing Your Session

AJ emphasizes the tangible "corporeality" of both Mary's service to Jesus, and Jesus's service to his disciples. She also writes that such service "becomes muscle memory; it is something we do, ideally on a regular basis, rather than merely think about."

Start planning a bodily act of service your group can do together. Perhaps you will cook a meal for a local homeless shelter. Perhaps you will pack food that will be sent overseas. Perhaps you will walk to raise funds for and awareness of mental health issues. Whatever you choose, make sure it is something that requires you and your participants to use your bodies. Also make sure group members with physical challenges or limitations can take part in some way. Bodily service need not be physically strenuous service, and even simply being physically present with others can be service.

## Closing Prayer

*Lord Jesus, you command us to love one another as you have loved us. May generous and humble service become "muscle memory" to us, that we may always truly live and move in this world as your body. Amen.*

## Optional Extensions

- "John makes us think about how and where we want to invest," writes AJ. Research what financial investments your congregation holds. How closely do you think these investments align with your faith? with love of God and neighbor? Are there any investment changes you would recommend? Why?

- If your congregation does not practice foot washing—whether on Holy (Maundy) Thursday or at some other time—explore doing so with your pastoral and worship leadership. What logistical arrangements will you need to make? How will you educate and prepare the congregation for the experience? How will you give worshippers opportunity to reflect on the experience afterward?
- Listen to settings of, and/or sing together, "Ubi Caritas," an ancient hymn traditionally sung during foot washing services. What makes this hymn appropriate for the occasion? Where do you find charity and love—and so, God—present today? (https://hymnary.org/text/ubi_caritas _et_amor)

# SESSION 6

# Mary Magdalene and Doubting Thomas

## (John 20)

### Session Goals

This session's reading, reflection, discussion, and prayer will help participants:

- explore the resurrection stories in John 20 from a variety of perspectives,
- apply insights from Mary Magdalene's and Thomas's encounters with the risen Jesus to their own and their congregation's belief and practice, and
- reflect on their experience of studying John's Gospel together.

### Biblical Foundations

*Early on the first day of the week, while it was still dark, Mary Magdalene came to the tomb and saw that the stone had been removed from the tomb. So she ran and went to Simon Peter and the other disciple, the one whom Jesus loved, and said to them, "They have taken the Lord out of the tomb, and we do not know where they have laid him." Then Peter and the other disciple set out and went toward the tomb. The two were running together, but the other disciple outran*

*Peter and reached the tomb first. He bent down to look in and saw the linen wrappings lying there, but he did not go in. Then Simon Peter came, following him, and went into the tomb. He saw the linen wrappings lying there, and the cloth that had been on Jesus's head, not lying with the linen wrappings but rolled up in a place by itself. Then the other disciple, who reached the tomb first, also went in, and he saw and believed, for as yet they did not understand the scripture, that he must rise from the dead. Then the disciples returned to their homes.*

*But Mary stood weeping outside the tomb. As she wept, she bent over to look into the tomb, and she saw two angels in white sitting where the body of Jesus had been lying, one at the head and the other at the feet. They said to her, "Woman, why are you weeping?" She said to them, "They have taken away my Lord, and I do not know where they have laid him." When she had said this, she turned around and saw Jesus standing there, but she did not know that it was Jesus. Jesus said to her, "Woman, why are you weeping? Whom are you looking for?" Supposing him to be the gardener, she said to him, "Sir, if you have carried him away, tell me where you have laid him, and I will take him away." Jesus said to her, "Mary!" She turned and said to him in Hebrew, "Rabbouni!" (which means Teacher). Jesus said to her, "Do not touch me, because I have not yet ascended to the Father. But go to my brothers and say to them, 'I am ascending to my Father and your Father, to my God and your God.'" Mary Magdalene went and announced to the disciples, "I have seen the Lord," and she told them that he had said these things to her.*

*John 20:1-18*

*When it was evening on that day, the first day of the week, and the doors were locked where the disciples were, for fear of the Jews, Jesus came and stood among them and said, "Peace be with you." After he said this, he showed them his hands and his side. Then the disciples rejoiced when they saw the Lord. Jesus said to them again, "Peace be with you. As the Father has sent me, so I send you." When he had said this, he breathed on them and said to them, "Receive the Holy Spirit. If you forgive the sins of any, they are forgiven them; if you retain the sins of any, they are retained."*

*But Thomas (who was called the Twin), one of the twelve, was not with them when Jesus came. So the other disciples told him, "We have seen the Lord." But he said to them, "Unless I see the mark of the nails in his hands and put my finger in the mark of the nails and my hand in his side, I will not believe."*

*A week later his disciples were again in the house, and Thomas was with them. Although the doors were shut, Jesus came and stood among them and said, "Peace be with you." Then he said to Thomas, "Put your finger here and see my hands. Reach out your hand and put it in my side. Do not doubt but believe." Thomas answered him, "My Lord and my God!" Jesus said to him, "Have you believed because you have seen me? Blessed are those who have not seen and yet have come to believe."*

*John 20:19-29*

## Before Your Session

- Carefully and prayerfully read this session's Biblical Foundation more than once. Note words and phrases that attract your attention, and meditate on them. Write down questions you have, and try to answer them, consulting trusted Bible commentaries. Become as familiar with these Scriptures as possible.
- Carefully read the introduction and chapter 6 of AJ's book more than once.
- You will need: either Bibles for in-person participants or screen slides prepared with Scripture texts for sharing (identify the translation used), or both; newsprint or a markerboard and markers (for in-person sessions).
- If using the DVD or streaming video, preview the session 6 video segment. Choose the best time in your session plan for viewing it.
- Consider whether you want to form two groups of participants for this session, assigning one group to study John 20:1-18 and the other John 20:19-29, each reporting

to the other before the session ends; or whether you will study both stories with the whole group.

## Starting Your Session

Welcome participants. Thank them for their participation in this study of John as guided by AJ's book. Remind them this session is the last session. Before you begin, ask volunteers to talk briefly about something they have learned or will remember most from the study, or about a question they still have.

## Opening Prayer

*Living God, who raised Jesus from death: As we gather once more to study John's Gospel, may your Spirit help us hear Christ call us by name, as his individual disciples and as his beloved community, that we may believe his good news and be able to tell others, with our lips and our lives, that we have seen the Lord! Amen.*

## Watch Session Video

Watch the session 6 video segment together. Discuss:

- Which of AJ's statements most interested, intrigued, surprised, or confused you? Why?
- What questions does this video segment raise for you?

## Book Discussion Questions

### *Mary and the Risen Jesus*

Recruit volunteers to read aloud John 20:1-18, taking the roles of the narrator, Mary, the two angels, and Jesus. Discuss:

- How does John's temporal note in verse 1 echo the beginnings of both his Gospel and Genesis? How does the day of this story become a "first day" for Mary, and for all Jesus's followers, apart from being the first day on the weekly calendar? How, as AJ writes, can every day both be "day one" and give us new perspectives on days that came before?

- How does Mary Magdalene's first appearance in John, at 19:25, inform our understanding of her role in this story?

- AJ notes Mary's name could be read as "Mary the Tower." How might this moniker be either appropriate or inappropriate, or both, for Mary? How does the traditional reading "Magdalene" reinforce AJ's assertion, "Each time Jesus sets foot in a location, it becomes something new"?

- What symbolic significance, if any, do you find in Mary's coming to Jesus's tomb "while it was still dark"?

- Who do you think are the "they" and "we" Mary refers to in verse 2? Why?

- How and why does Mary's initial report to Peter and the Beloved Disciple develop the "come and see" motif in John's Gospel (see 1:39, 46; 4:29; 11:34)?

- AJ says John's Gospel suggests a rivalry between Peter and the Beloved Disciple. What significance, if any, do you find in their run to Jesus's tomb and the Beloved Disciple not entering the tomb before Peter? When, if ever, have you experienced rivalries in your faith community, and how did you handle them?

- AJ calls the small cloth rolled up by itself in verse 7 a "clue" to Jesus's resurrection. How so? Do you discover "clues" to Jesus's resurrection in your life? in your community? in the world? If so, what and where are they? If not, why not?

- What does the Beloved Disciple believe at the tomb (v. 8) if neither he nor Peter understands the Scriptures as pointing to Jesus's resurrection (v. 9)? Does their response to Jesus's empty tomb in verse 10 compare favorably, unfavorably, or neither to Mary's response? Why?

- As AJ notes, verse 11 "is not the first time in [John's] Gospel we have seen a woman named Mary weep at a tomb."

Compare John 11:32-35. How, if at all, do the two scenes interpret each other?

- AJ notes, "We each encounter death, and mourning, in our own way." And, "Hope, indeed surety, of resurrection does not make the loss easier." Have you ever been criticized for how you mourned a loss? How did you respond or how might you respond differently now?
- Why does Mary see more in Jesus's tomb than Peter and the Beloved Disciple saw? chance and timing? divine will? openness to seeing more? some other reason?
- Why do the angels sit where Jesus's head and feet had been (v. 12)? How does their presence interpret John 1:21, which AJ notes is "the only other reference to angels in [John's] Gospel"?
- The angels address Mary as "woman," which AJ states echoes other addresses to "woman" in John's Gospel (2:4; 4:21; 19:26). How do these other addresses to "woman" shape your understanding of this story?
- AJ notes it isn't clear Mary recognizes she is seeing angels. What do you think? Do you think the angels' question to her is a genuine one? Why or why not?
- John does make clear Mary doesn't immediately recognize Jesus (v. 14). Why doesn't she? Why does Jesus ask Mary why she weeps (v. 15)?
- AJ explains that the way John narrates Mary's encounter with Jesus evokes a common motif of separated lovers and mistaken identity from stories in the ancient Greek-speaking world. Why might John have chosen to tell this story as he does? How and why does this meeting of a woman and man in a garden also evoke the story of Eden in Genesis 2–3?
- What is the significance of Jesus calling Mary by name (v. 16; see also 10:3)? How do biblical echoes of Mary's name (Miriam) add depth to the story? When, if ever, have you felt as though Jesus called you by name?

- How do other addresses of Jesus as "rabbi" in John's Gospel add meaning to Mary's calling Jesus "Rabbouni" ("my teacher") (1:38, 49; 3:2, 26; 4:31; 6:25; 9:2; 11:18)?
- Why does Jesus tell Mary not to touch him (see also 14:26; 16:5-7)? What does he commission her to do instead? Does Jesus's prohibition to not "hold on to" him apply to his followers today? If so, how? If not, why not?
- Why doesn't John record the disciples' response to Mary's announcement (v. 18)? What is the "long-term commission," in AJ's words, Mary must still fulfill after fulfilling her "immediate responsibility"? What immediate and long-term responsibilities fall to Jesus's disciples today because of the announcement of his resurrection?

### *Thomas and the Risen Jesus*

Recruit volunteers to read aloud John 20:19-29, taking the roles of the narrator, Jesus, the disciples, and Thomas. Discuss:

- Thomas's name means "twin," and AJ mentions speculation from texts not in the New Testament that Thomas might have been Judas Iscariot's or even Jesus's twin. How do Jesus's followers run the risk of being Judas's "twin"? How do they best live as Jesus's "twin"?
- AJ explains some early Christian traditions connected with Thomas sought salvation in secret "knowledge" (*gnōsis*) about Jesus, rather than in his bodily crucifixion and resurrection. Why is Thomas, then, "the perfect figure" for the story in John 20? When and how, if ever, do Christians today value knowledge over trust, faith, and belief in Jesus?
- In John's Gospel, Thomas has previously appeared at 11:14-16 and 14:1-7. What, if anything, can we tell about Thomas that might help us understand his story in John 20?

- AJ points out that the disciples' "fear of the Jews" (v. 19) is inaccurate, since Jesus and his first disciples were Jews. Accepting John's statement at face value can also perpetuate anti-Jewish readings of the New Testament. "Mary Magdalene was not hiding," AJ points out, "so why are [the disciples]"? What do you think? When have you been afraid to speak or act in Jesus's name, despite the news of the Resurrection? What about your congregation?
- Why are shut and locked doors no barrier to Jesus (see also 10:7-10)?
- Why is Jesus's greeting of peace (vv. 19, 21, 26) surprising? Why is it welcome? When have you received an unexpected but welcome greeting of peace? When did you last extend such a greeting?
- Why does Jesus show his hands and side to his disciples (v. 20)? Why does the resurrected Jesus still bear the marks of his suffering and death? What marks, literal or otherwise, do you bear from your past that, in part, make you who you are, but do not define you?
- What does Jesus sending his followers as the Father sent him specifically mean (v. 21)? How and why is the Holy Spirit (v. 22) connected to this sending?
- What does it mean for Jesus's disciples to forgive sins and retain (v. 23)? How does your community exercise this responsibility?
- Why doesn't John mention Thomas's absence until verse 24? How proactively do you look for those who are missing from your congregation? What do you do when they are missing?
- AJ thinks Thomas "should have been primed" by virtue of what he saw as a disciple of Jesus. Yet Thomas wants to see what the other disciples have already seen (v. 20). What do you think about Thomas's criterion for believing the announcement of Jesus's resurrection? What is the significance of Jesus offering to meet it (v. 27)?

- How is Thomas's confession of faith personal rather than abstract, and experiential rather than creedal (v. 28)?

## Closing Your Session

AJ sometimes encourages Christians (who often ask her why she does not "believe in Jesus") to ask themselves, "Why do you believe in Jesus?" "What exactly do you believe?" "How does this belief guide your life?" "The answer need not be a matter of 'proof' such as what Thomas demanded," she says; "it may rather be a matter of what the heart says, a matter of where love and peace can be found."

Invite volunteers to talk briefly about one or more of the three questions AJ raises. Be ready to start discussion by doing so yourself. After all who wish to share have shared, thank all group members again for participating in this study of John's Gospel and of AJ's book.

## Closing Prayer

*Now send us again, risen Christ, as your Father and ours, your God and ours, sent you: into the world in love and service. Breathe your Spirit on us again, that we may remain your obedient siblings, shining with your light, which no darkness can overcome. Amen.*

## Optional Extension

- Read and discuss John 21, referring to AJ's commentary on the story in her book's epilogue.

# About the
# Leader Guide Writer

**The Rev. Michael S. Poteet** is an ordained Minister of Word and Sacrament in the Presbyterian Church (U.S.A.). A graduate of the College of William and Mary and Princeton Theological Seminary, he serves the larger church as a Christian education writer, biblical storyteller, and guest preacher. You can find his occasional musings on the meetings of faith and fiction at http://www.bibliomike.com.

**Watch videos based
on *The Gospel of John:
A Beginner's Guide to
the Way, the Truth,
and the Life*
with Amy-Jill Levine
through Amplify Media.**

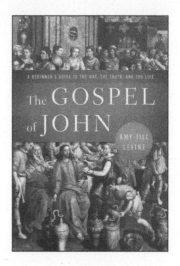

*Amplify Media* is a multimedia platform that delivers high-quality, searchable content with an emphasis on Wesleyan perspectives for churchwide, group, or individual use on any device at any time. In a world of sometimes overwhelming choices, Amplify gives church leaders and congregants media capabilities that are contemporary, relevant, effective, and, most important, affordable and sustainable.

With *Amplify Media* church leaders can:

- Provide a reliable source of Christian content through a Wesleyan lens for teaching, training, and inspiration in a customizable library
- Deliver their own preaching and worship content in a way the congregation knows and appreciates
- Build the church's capacity to innovate with engaging content and accessible technology
- Equip the congregation to better understand the Bible and its application
- Deepen discipleship beyond the church walls

**Ask your group leader or pastor about Amplify Media
and sign up today at www.AmplifyMedia.com.**

Milton Keynes UK
Ingram Content Group UK Ltd.
UKHW041823240724
446079UK00004B/52